When It Hurts To Believe

Nash de los Santos

Copyright © 2025 Nash de los Santos

All rights reserved. No part of this book may be reproduced, stored in a retrieval system, or transmitted in any form or by any means, including electronic, mechanical, photocopying, recording, or otherwise, without the prior written permission of the author. The only exception is brief quotations used in reviews or articles.

The stories, reflections, and insights in this book are shared from the author's personal experience and Christian faith. While great care has been taken in presenting the material, the author assumes no responsibility for any errors or omissions.

Printed in the United Kingdom.

Cover design by: Nash Delos Santos

Interior design by: Noble Legacy Publishing

ISBN: 978-1-911761-33-4

Dedication

To **Riza**,

my wife, my faithful companion, who never stopped praying even when I stopped believing.

Your quiet strength, unwavering love, and deep faith have carried me through the darkest valleys.

You led me back to God without ever raising your voice just by being who you are.

And to **Shann**, my beloved son,

you are the reason I choose to keep walking forward, even when the road is painful.

Every word in this book is a step I take for you.

May you one day see how even brokenness can become beautiful when surrendered to God's hands.

You both are my greatest blessings, and the living proof that love always leads home.

AUTHOR'S NOTE

I didn't write this book as someone who's already healed.

I wrote it as someone who's still healing.

This is not a manual on how to overcome pain. It's not a step-by-step guide on how to pray your way out of suffering. What you'll find here are pieces of my own story, raw, imperfect, unfinished. These pages hold the tears I didn't always know how to cry, the questions I didn't always know how to ask, and the grace I didn't always recognise until much later.

I grew up Catholic, studied philosophy and theology, even entered the seminary. But none of that stopped me from falling apart. None of it shielded me from doubt, depression, loss, and spiritual dryness. What I've learned is that no one is exempt from pain, not even the faithful. Maybe especially not the faithful.

But I've also learned this: our wounds, when surrendered to God, become sacred. They may not go away, but they can be transformed. They can become bridges instead of walls. They can become vessels of compassion and understanding. Both for ourselves and for others.

If you're reading this as someone who's in the middle of the valley please know that I see you. More importantly, God sees you. This book is for you.

I wrote it for the believer who feels numb. For the one who shows up to church with a tired soul. For the parent who silently suffers. For the leader who feels unseen. For the man or woman who no longer knows how to pray. For anyone who still loves God but feels too broken to say it out loud.

I wrote this for the father who carries the weight of his children's struggles and silently wishes in his heart if only he could bear their pain instead. I wrote this for the men who long to be better husbands but believe that money in the bank matters more than flowers and chocolates ever could. I wrote this for the leaders who have poured out their hearts in service, yet see no visible fruit or that everything doesn't seem to be moving ahead. I wrote this for every member who is faithfully serving, even while facing misunderstanding or persecution from those entrusted with leadership.

My prayer is that, through these pages, you'll find something that resonates. A word. A story. A scripture. A moment of peace in the storm.

Thank you for giving me your time and your trust. Thank you for letting my story touch yours.

Above all, may you never forget that you are loved and you are not alone.

And God, no matter how silent He seems, is still with you.

This book isn't just a story. It's an invitation.

Each section begins with a reflection or experience drawn from my own journey, and ends with a moment I call **Grace in the Silence**, a space to pause, pray, and ponder.

You'll find scripture, reflection questions, and prompts that I hope will help you go deeper, not just into my story, but into your own. If you're holding this book in your hands, I pray you won't just read it… but wrestle with it, rest in it, and let it speak to the quiet places in you that long to be seen and healed.

Bring a journal, or just an open heart. God will meet you there.

OPENING PRAYER

Before You Begin

Take a breath. Quiet your heart.

Let this prayer guide you into sacred space.

Lord, my God,

I come before You not with perfect words but with an open heart.

I bring my pain, my doubts, my silence, and I lay them down before You.

As I turn these pages,
help me not just to read, but to listen

Speak to me in the stories,
whisper in the silence
,and breathe Your truth into the wounds I carry.

May every section of this book
become a space where I meet You
in honesty, in grace, and in hope.

Let Your Spirit accompany me in this journey.
And if I find healing here,

may it lead me to healing others too.

I pray this in Jesus' name.

Amen.

PROLOGUE

Pain has a way of changing people. It slows you down, shuts you in, makes you question even the things you once held certain. Pain can destroy the very foundation you once held dear or carefully built. It can tear through marriages, break your heart in an instant, and drive your mind into dark places you never thought you'd go. It doesn't matter how strong you think you are. Sometimes, even the strongest among us find themselves in the most painful situations. I know this, not just from stories I've heard, but from the life I've lived.

There were days I stood on the edge of belief, days when the silence of God felt louder than any answer. I've been through the kind of pain that doesn't just bruise the body but aches in the soul. The kind of pain that wakes you up in the middle of the night, not from noise, but from a heaviness of the beating of the heart. The kind of pain that slowly breaks your heart where you can almost hear every fibre snap. And your mind trying to shield your heart from further harm, ends up blocking out the triggers but also shattering your sense of self and confidence in the process.

At some point, I began to wonder: *Why does God allow suffering, especially to those who are trying their best to love Him?* I asked this not as a theologian, not even as a servant of the faith, but as a father, a husband, a brother, a son. As someone who has buried loved ones too soon, lost things I worked hard for, and watched people I deeply care for wrestle in silence.

I didn't set out to write a book. I set out to survive.

But the Lord has a way of bringing something purposeful out of our pain. And slowly, through reflection, prayer, and the people He placed around me, I began to understand that pain, though unwelcome, was not meaningless. That somehow, in the brokenness, God was still working. And even when I couldn't see it, He was reshaping my life from the inside out.

This book is not a how-to guide on escaping pain. It's not a list of quick fixes or religious clichés. It's a walk-through. A companionship in the valley.

It's me saying to you, *"You are not alone."* I wrote this for those who are grieving. For those who are angry.

For those who are numb, and for those still searching for answers. I wrote this for the faithful who feel like God has gone silent. And for the doubters who are too tired to keep pretending.

This book is my offering. It's my way of sitting beside you in your sorrow and sharing how pain has shaped my own journey. Both the tears and the healing, the silence and the grace.

And if this book leads even one heart back to hope, then every word will have been worth it.

ABOUT THE AUTHOR

Nash Delos Santos is a Catholic husband, father, and servant whose journey of faith has been shaped by seasons of doubt, pain, and redemption. Once a seminarian who walked away from the Church, Nash spent years wrestling with God through the death of loved ones, spiritual dryness, personal collapse, marital problems and depression.

But grace is persistent.

Through a powerful reawakening of faith, Nash found his way back to God and to the Church by walking straight through the fire of suffering. Today, he shares his testimony through writing, speaking, and service. He serves as a servant-leader in Couples for Christ in Cardiff, United Kingdom, alongside his wife, Riza, while raising their son, Shann.

When not writing or ministering, Nash enjoys quiet walks, deep conversations, and spending time with his son, Shann, his greatest earthly blessing and the source of much of his strength. He also writes code for CFC and other projects, using his skills to support missions that matter.

"When It Hurts to Believe" is his first Christian book, a collection of years of journaling, a spiritual memoir born from silence, struggle, and the unwavering pursuit of God in the dark.

Table of Contents

CHAPTER 1 1
   1.1 The Many Faces of Pain 3
   1.2 Why Does It Hurt So Much 5
   1.3 The Gift Of Silence 9
   1.4 Pain Can Reveal What Comfort Hides 13
   1.5 Jesus Did Not Avoid Pain 18
   1.6 The Beginning Of The Journey 22

CHAPTER 2 26
   2.1 The Unavoidable Question 28
   2.2 The Mystery of God's Will 32
   2.3 Jesus Didn't Answer It, He Entered It 36
   2.4 Saints Who Suffered Well 40
   2.5 Faith Doesn't Eliminate the Question But It Changes the Journey 44

CHAPTER 3 48
   3.1 The Lie Of Comfort Culture 50
   3.2 Pain as the Furnace of Growth 53
   3.3 The Cross Is Not Optional And Our Mother Knows The Way 57
   3.4 There Is No Resurrection Without the Cross 63
   3.5 When We Don't Feel Strong Enough 67

CHAPTER 4 72

   4.1 Start Where You Are 74

   4.2 The Power of Prayer When It's Hard to Pray 78

   4.3 Anchored in the Sacraments 83

   4.4 Let People In 88

   4.5 Carrying Pain With Purpose 92

   4.6 Give Yourself Permission to Rest 96

   4.7 When You Ask God for Something 101

CHAPTER 1
WHAT IS PAIN, REALLY?

Pain. Most of us try to avoid it, push it away, or wonder why it even has to be part of our lives. But if we slow down and take a closer look, pain isn't just something we feel. It's trying to tell us something. It's a signal. A message. Sometimes, it's even a doorway to something deeper.

A pain can be a sign that something is not right. It's a signal to let you know that something is brewing and it tells you to pay attention. It's the body's way of waking us up to something deeper, something unresolved, something that needs our care. And sometimes it can also be the soul's way of telling us that's something essential needs attention.

We usually think of pain in physical terms like a broken bone, an illness, an injury. But the most profound kinds of pain often leave no visible marks. The ache of losing a loved one. The sting of betrayal. The silent weight of depression or loneliness. These are wounds of the heart and soul, and they can hurt even more than what the body endures.

1.1
The Many Faces of Pain

Pain shows up in our lives wearing different faces. There's the sudden, sharp jolt of physical pain, could be from an accident, an illness, a diagnosis that changes everything. Then there's the slower, quieter ache of emotional wounds brought about by grief, rejection, loneliness, the pain of waiting.

Sometimes, the most devastating kind of pain is spiritual. The kind that makes us cry out, "Where is God in this?" It's the silence we feel in prayer, the sense of abandonment, the fear that our suffering has no meaning.

There was a time in my life when I stopped praying to God. Not out of rebellion, but out of resignation. I began to think prayer was pointless. That maybe, all the time I spent kneeling and hoping would've been better spent on improving myself, growing my skills, or advancing my career. At least then I'd see some results, I thought. I began to believe that no one, not even God, could truly change my life but me.

This wasn't dramatic or loud at all. It was subtle and quiet. I still went through the motions. I still believed, at least intellectually. But spiritually, I felt numb. It was a slow drifting, not a sudden departure. And in that silence, I didn't feel peace. I felt hollow.

Even though I was still going to Mass, still praying, it felt like I was

shouting into a void. That kind of pain doesn't leave bruises, but it bruises the soul.

And yet, this is not unique to me. Many faithful Catholics, priests, religious, married couples, even saints have walked through similar valleys.

That's the thing about pain, it doesn't always show up the way we expect. Sometimes it takes the form of spiritual dryness, or emotional fatigue. Sometimes it looks like success on the outside, but deep down, it's fuelled by fear, anxiety, or the need to escape something we haven't named yet.

Understanding pain means being honest with what it looks like in our own lives.

It means looking beyond the obvious and acknowledging the subtle wounds. Those ones that we ignore because we've grown used to them.

Before we can heal, we have to name the pain.

Before we can move forward, we have to stop pretending we're not hurting.

I guess the first step is to acknowledge the pain and what causes it. Instead of denying it or hiding it away, we need to face it and to recognise that it's there, and to be brave enough to ask what's really behind it. Not just the effects we feel, but the root causes we often avoid.

1.2
Why Does It Hurt So Much

Pain strikes at our vulnerability. It reminds us that we're not in control. That's part of what makes it so difficult.

Sometimes, we try to fix the pain by distracting ourselves and by indulging in things that usually bring us happiness, thinking it might help ease the ache. We turn to food, entertainment, shopping, or even constant busyness, hoping it'll dull whatever hurts inside. But no matter what we do, the pain is still there. Why? Because we're often applying the wrong solutions. And when those quick fixes don't work, we end up feeling even more frustrated… sometimes more broken than before.

But if we look through the lens of faith, we begin to understand something deeper. Pain is not just a curse or a punishment. In fact, Catholic teaching reminds us that suffering entered the world through sin (original sin), but God did not abandon us to it. He entered into it Himself.

St. Paul speaks of a mysterious "thorn in the flesh" (2 Corinthians 12:7), something painful that he begged God to take away. But the Lord answered, *"My grace is sufficient for you, for power is made perfect in weakness."*

That single line holds so much. It tells us that pain can become a place where grace abounds. Not because the pain itself is good, but because God can work even there.

We hurt so much because pain touches what we value most. Like our relationships, our dreams, our sense of worth and identity. When something we love is threatened or lost, the ache can feel unbearable. That's why emotional and spiritual pain often run deeper than physical wounds. They affect how we see ourselves, how we see God, and how we relate to others.

I remember a moment when this truth hit me with crushing force.

The place was Buffalo, NY, in a Chinese restaurant just a couple of turns from Niagara Falls. We were joking around, laughing like it was any other day. Then her phone rang, her doctor calling. It was barely a minute-long call, but it changed everything. She put the phone down, her hands visibly shaking and with a blank look said, "I have ovarian cancer."

Silence.

The restaurant, once warm and noisy, suddenly felt cold and massive and hollow. No one knew what to say. We offered comforting words, but deep down I knew that it wouldn't help. I couldn't even process my own feelings, let alone imagine the weight she must have been carrying.

Her name was Maria Paz. She was the third in our family of six siblings. I'm the second. Her name means "beloved" and "peace". A name that somehow carried both tenderness and strength. And that's exactly who she was.

The trip back to the UK felt longer than usual. I didn't want to leave her like that. Over the next few months, things got worse. When we visited again in December, I wasn't sure if it was the right decision but I had to see her.

She was fading. Once radiant and full of life, now fragile like a wilting petal. Watching her move, seeing her in pain tore my heart into pieces of aches. And though I physically returned home to the UK, I left something behind. My heart, my strength, my sense of direction.

I stopped speaking. I started sleeping in another room. Even my wife's touch, once comforting, now felt like a burden. I drowned myself in work, not to be productive, but just to escape. I'd stare at the computer screen for hours, numb and lost. Eventually, I got fired from the job I loved. And at the same time, the bond in our marriage began to fray. Yet, we still served the community. Every week, we travelled long hours to attend household gatherings. We didn't talk much in the car. And when we did, it often ended in arguments. Our son would listen quietly from the backseat, sometimes telling us to stop. We smiled in front of people, but inside, I was falling apart. I had never felt so alone... so useless... so lost.

That was the first time I truly understood what depression felt like.

And just when I thought I couldn't feel any lower, it got worse. One night, after a meeting, everything shattered. I was shamed, and rejected by someone I deeply respected. Someone who knew what I was going through, yet offered no compassion, only expectations, criticisms,

and harsh words. I broke. I curled up in the corner of the sofa, shaking uncontrollably. I cried like a child who had lost everything. My world had gone dark, and I couldn't find a way out.

Pain exposes our limits. It humbles us. It shows us that we're not selfsufficient, even when we try to be. And in that vulnerability, we're invited to turn to the One who *is* sufficient. As uncomfortable as it is, pain strips away illusions and reveals what we truly depend on. Sometimes, that revelation hurts more than the pain itself.

There's also a mystery to pain that we won't fully understand in this life. And that's part of the struggle. It hurts so much because it often feels senseless. We cry out, "*Why me?*" or "*Why now?*" hoping for clarity. But what we get instead is silence… or at best, a whisper of grace that says, *"I'm with you."* And honestly, that doesn't always feel like enough.

We're not called to *understand* suffering as much as we're called to *unite* it with Christ. Jesus didn't avoid pain but He wilfully entered it, fully. He wept. He sweat blood. He cried out from the Cross, "*My God, my God, why have You forsaken Me?*" That cry doesn't mean He lost faith, it means He understands ours.

And maybe that's why it hurts so much: because we were never meant to carry it alone. Pain becomes unbearable when we try to manage it apart from grace. But when we offer it up, when we let Christ carry it with us, it doesn't always get easier… but it becomes redemptive.

1.3
The Gift Of Silence

We don't always need explanations. Sometimes, what we need is God's presence. And the presence of people who walk with us.

Some pains don't come with a neat reason. A child is born with an illness. A loving spouse passes away unexpectedly. A dedicated servant of the Church falls into deep depression. We want answers. And often, we don't get them.

For me, that season came during the height of COVID. Strangely, it wasn't the virus that hit me hardest. It was everything else that came rushing in all at once. The loss of my sister and the loss of my job pulled me into a quiet kind of depression, one I didn't fully recognise at first but that slowly began to affect everything especially my marriage and my relationships with others.

All I wanted was to be left alone. I avoided conversations, not because I didn't care, but because I couldn't bear to face what those conversations might bring. I didn't want to settle the issues, because deep down, I was terrified that I wouldn't be able to stand if I tried. I feared that facing the truth about my grief, my failures and my pain would be too much. I didn't just fear losing people… I feared losing myself. I couldn't even confront my own heart without feeling like everything might fall apart.

I didn't stop believing in God. But I did stop speaking to Him.

Prayer felt pointless. I remember thinking, *what's the use?* it just felt like everything I said to Him was falling on deaf ears. I felt spiritually dry, and being with someone, even my spouse, didn't feel like comfort anymore. All I wanted was to be left alone. That isolation wasn't just physical; it was emotional, even spiritual.

And yet... healing found its way in.

It wasn't theology that pulled me back. It was because of a small moment. Someone lighting a candle for me in church. They didn't say anything. They probably didn't even realise how much I was hurting. But that simple act, though quiet, gentle but intentional, broke something open in me. It reminded me that even when I couldn't speak to God, He had not stopped reaching out to me.

It was only later that I found out Riza, together with the sisters in the community, had been constantly praying for me. While I was withdrawing into silence, they were lifting me up in theirs. Their prayers became a quiet bridge between my pain and God's presence. One I didn't even know I was walking across.

It reminded me that even in silence, God listens. And even when I feel too tired to pray, the prayers of others hold me up.

I've come to see that silence itself can be a gift. Not a void, but a

sacred space where healing can begin. Silence allows the soul to breathe, to cry out without words, to be still before God without needing to perform or explain. It's in the silence that we often become most honest about our fears, our questions, and our need for mercy.

Even Jesus, in His most painful moments, embraced silence. He was silent before His accusers. Silent in the Garden as He sweat blood. Silent on the Cross, except for a few agonizing words. His silence wasn't weakness. It was surrender. It was strength. It was sacred.

Scripture reminds us that God often speaks not through wind or fire, but in the gentle whisper (1 Kings 19:12). And in that whisper, we're reminded: even in silence, we are seen. We are held. We are loved.

So if you ever find yourself in a season of silence, don't rush to fill it. Don't panic because God seems quiet. Sometimes, the silence is where He's doing His deepest work.

Grace In The Silence

"The Lord is close to the broken-hearted, and saves those who are crushed in spirit."

Psalm 34:18

There are moments when our pain feels invisible even to those closest to us. But God sees it all. This psalm reminds us that His presence is not withdrawn during suffering; in fact, He draws even closer. When we feel forgotten, abandoned, or too broken to speak, God is not far. He is near, holding us gently even in silence.

1.4
Pain Can Reveal What Comfort Hides

Comfort isn't bad. It's natural to desire ease, peace, and joy in life. God Himself created the world for our good, and He delights when we are blessed.

But comfort has a subtle danger: it can lull us into thinking we have everything we need. When life is running smoothly, we can begin to rely on ourselves without even noticing. We might still pray, still go to Mass, but underneath it all, we might not be depending on God. Not really.

Pain has a way of breaking through that illusion.

It strips away our defences, our pride, our carefully constructed routines. And in the stillness that follows, when all the noise is gone, we begin to hear things we never heard before.

Sometimes, pain is the only thing that slows us down enough to really listen.

I remember speaking with a man who had been very successful in his career, well respected, always in control. But when he lost his job unexpectedly, followed by a serious health diagnosis, everything changed. He told me later, *"I used to pray because it was part of my routine. But in the hospital, I prayed because I had nothing else. And that was the first time I think I really meant it."*

That's not to say God causes these things just to get our attention. But He allows them, and through them, He works. Pain can bring us face to face with our true selves and our deepest need for grace.

Pain exposes the attachments and comforts we've unknowingly idolised. It reveals how often we cling to things for our security that were never meant to bear that weight. When comfort is taken away, we're often surprised to discover just how dependent we had become on it, not only for happiness, but for identity.

But here's the strange and holy paradox: it's in those moments of loss that we find something more solid. A foundation that doesn't shake. A peace that doesn't rely on circumstances. In losing what comfort hides, we often discover what truly matters.

It can also make us more compassionate. Those who have walked through deep valleys are often the first to recognise someone else in pain. They become gentler, slower to judge, and more willing to sit with others in silence.

Comfort rarely teaches us that. But pain often does.

Pope Benedict XVI once said something powerful:

"The world offers you comfort, but you were not made for comfort. You were made for greatness."

Greatness, in the Christian sense, isn't about success or praise. It's about becoming fully alive in Christ. Something that often comes not through ease, but through endurance.

It's forged in the fire of trials, not in the cushions of comfort.

Pain also reveals the hidden judgments we carry or endure from others.

Some of the most painful wounds aren't physical or even circumstantial. They're relational. They come from the comments, assumptions, or misunderstandings of people we thought would understand.

Most of our friends including those in our Couples for Christ community have, at one point or another, questioned us about our son Shann. Some even partly blamed us for the way he is. They've suggested that perhaps we spent too much time serving, and not enough focusing on each other or on him. That maybe if we had poured more into our careers or our marriage, things might have turned out differently.

And while I understand that those words may have come from concern, they still hurt deeply. Because what they didn't see was how much love, time, and prayer we have poured into our family. They didn't see the quiet sacrifices, the long conversations, the tears behind closed doors. We have already offered our lives and our service to God. We've trusted Him with everything, including our son.

That doesn't mean we've been perfect, and it certainly doesn't mean we've neglected our responsibilities. Far from it. But pain has shown us something comfort never could: that obedience to God doesn't always look like success to others. Sometimes, faithfulness means standing firm even when misunderstood and trusting that God's plan is still good, even when it doesn't look like what people expect.

In the ache of being judged, we learned to let go of the need for others' approval.

In the quiet grief of being misunderstood, we clung more fiercely to the One who sees everything clearly.

Pain reveals what comfort hides: that we are not enough on our own. And that's not a flaw. It's an invitation.

An invitation to trust more deeply, to love more selflessly, and to cling to Christ more firmly.

And in that way, pain doesn't just expose our weakness but it leads us to the source of our true strength.

Grace In The Silence

"Before I was afflicted I went astray, but now I keep your word."

Psalm 119:67

Suffering has a way of turning our hearts back toward God. When things fall apart, we often discover how far we've drifted and how deeply we need His Word. Pain can become the doorway that brings us home again, not in punishment, but in mercy.

1.5
Jesus Did Not Avoid Pain

One of the most comforting truths of our faith is also the most startling: God Himself suffered.

Jesus didn't live a life free from pain. He wasn't shielded from sadness, betrayal, loneliness, or physical agony. In fact, His life was marked by suffering from beginning to end. Born in poverty. Rejected by His own people. Misunderstood, abandoned, falsely accused, mocked, tortured, and crucified.

If anyone had the right to avoid pain, it was Him. But He didn't.

Instead, He embraced it not passively, but deliberately. Jesus didn't just *experience* pain; He *chose* it. He walked toward the Cross, fully aware of what it would cost Him. Not because pain is good in itself, but because love is willing to suffer for the beloved. And He chose to suffer for us.

Not only did He endure physical torture, but He carried the crushing weight of our sin. As the prophet Isaiah foretold: *"He has borne our griefs and carried our sorrows"* (Isaiah 53:4). In Jesus, God didn't merely sympathise with our pain. Instead, He stepped into it completely, down to the darkest depths.

He entered into suffering so that it would never be a place we face alone.

Jesus cried. He sweat blood. He experienced the full weight of human anguish. One of the most haunting verses in Scripture is His cry on the Cross:

"My God, my God, why have you forsaken me?" (Matthew 27:46)

Even though He was God, He allowed Himself to experience the desolation we sometimes feel. And still, in His pain, He held fast to the Father.

Why would God do that?

Because He wanted to meet us in our most vulnerable places.

Because He knew we would need to see that He gets it not from a distance, but from the inside.

This is the mystery of redemptive suffering: that our pain, united with Christ's, can become a source of grace. Not only for us, but for others too. Our wounds, when offered in love, participate in His saving work. They don't become meaningless; they become holy.

I think of my mother. She died due to complications from diabetes, but the truth is, she had been suffering since I was young. I saw it up close. Her left leg had to be amputated. I can't even imagine how painful that must have been for her. She couldn't eat the food we all enjoyed.

Her ability to go places was limited. Her body bore both physical and emotional pain every single day.

And yet, what I saw in her wasn't bitterness. It was joy.

She lived with purpose. She went to church almost every day and never missed a Sunday Mass. She was actively involved in the Catholic Women's League and other small Church communities. She was generous, kind, and always thinking of others. And through it all, I don't remember hearing her complain.

She showed me that suffering does not define a person, faith does. That even a life marked by pain can become a living witness to the love and power of God.

This doesn't mean we have to enjoy suffering, or that we shouldn't pray for healing. Christ Himself prayed in the Garden of Gethsemane, *"Father, if it is possible, let this cup pass from me."* But He followed that with: *"Yet not as I will, but as you will."*

That surrender, painful and courageous, is what makes His suffering redemptive. It turns the Cross from a symbol of defeat into the greatest sign of love the world has ever known.

When we suffer, we are not asked to carry a different cross. We're invited to carry His and with Him. And in doing so, our suffering is transformed. Not erased, but transfigured. It becomes, mysteriously and beautifully, a path to glory.

Grace In The Silence

"For we do not have a high priest who is unable to sympathise with our weaknesses, but one who has similarly been tested in every way, yet without sin."

Hebrews 4:15

Jesus is not distant from your pain. He knows it. He has lived it. And because of that, He can walk with you through it. Not as a stranger, but as a Saviour who understands every tear, every silence, every ache.

1.6
The Beginning Of The Journey

Pain has a way of changing us. It forces us to stop, to see, to feel things we often try to avoid. And as uncomfortable as that can be, it also opens a doorway, a path where healing, meaning, and even holiness can begin to unfold.

By now, maybe you're seeing something stir in your own story. Maybe you're remembering a moment of pain that shaped you. Or maybe you're still in the thick of it, trying to find your footing. Wherever you are, know this: pain is not the end of your story. It might actually be the beginning.

That's what this journey is about.

This book isn't meant to offer easy answers or quick fixes. If that were possible, pain would've left us long ago. But there's something greater at work beneath the surface. Something sacred. When we approach pain not as a curse to escape but as a mystery to enter, we begin to see it differently. It becomes less about *why this is happening* and more about *what God is doing through it.*

Pain not only cracks open our hearts; it also clears our vision. It teaches us to see with new eyes. To notice things we once ignored. It makes room for depth, humility, and a longing for something eternal. This is why so many spiritual journeys begin not with clarity, but with confusion. Pain invites the kind of questions that comfort often suppresses.

Pain is a wilderness, yes. But God has been known to meet His people in the wilderness.

In Scripture, the desert is not just a place of testing but a place of encounter. God spoke to Moses in the burning bush. He sustained the Israelites with manna. He led them with fire and cloud. And when Jesus began His ministry, He too went into the desert.

So maybe you are in a kind of desert now. Or maybe someone you love is. That's okay. Because this isn't the end. It's the beginning.

But beginnings are rarely easy. They often require us to unlearn false stories, like the belief that suffering means God is absent, or that brokenness makes us less worthy. As we walk this road, we may discover that what we thought disqualified us from grace is actually the very place where grace wants to meet us.

And we don't walk alone. God not only walks with us. He often sends others to journey beside us. A spiritual friend. A priest. A small act of kindness from someone who doesn't even know our pain. Sometimes healing begins through a conversation, a gesture, or a prayer said quietly on our behalf. Community becomes the road we travel.

There is something on the other side of pain. But the way through is not to deny it or run from it. The way through is to walk it honestly, faithfully, and never alone.

Grace rarely rushes. It begins in small, quiet ways. A tear. A candle. A whispered prayer. A willingness to hope again. That, too, is the beginning of the journey.

Pain is complex. It wears many faces. Whether physical, emotional or spiritual. Each one can leave us feeling confused, broken, or abandoned. But as we've begun to see, pain is not meaningless. It reveals what comfort often hides: our need for healing, for hope, and most of all, for God.

We explored how pain can humble us, awaken us, and draw us into deeper communion with Christ who did not avoid suffering but embraced it out of love. We heard stories of people who carried pain with dignity and faith, showing us that even in the hardest seasons, grace is still possible.

We may not always understand *why* pain comes, but we now know it can be the start of a journey. One that doesn't end in despair, but in deeper trust.

And so, we walk forward not with all the answers, but with hearts more open to ask the right questions. We walk forward with Christ, who walks with us even when we cannot see Him.

The next step? Wrestling honestly with one of the biggest questions of all: If God is good, why does He allow suffering?

Grace In The Silence

"I will lead her into the wilderness and speak tenderly to her."

Hosea 2:14

God does not abandon us in the wilderness. He draws us there to speak to our hearts and not with shouts, but with a gentle, healing voice. The wilderness may feel like a place of loss, but in His hands, it becomes a place of love and transformation

CHAPTER 2

THE QUESTION OF WHY - PAIN AND GOD'S GOODNESS

When we're hurting, the most natural question we ask is: *Why?* Why this pain? Why now? Why me or why them? Beneath all these cries lies a deeper question still: *If God is good, then why does He allow suffering at all?* This is not just a philosophical riddle; it is a deeply personal and spiritual struggle. And for many believers, this tension becomes the very place where faith is tested, stretched, or sometimes, sadly, abandoned.

We know from Scripture and tradition that God is all-loving, all knowing, and all-powerful. So, when pain enters our lives, it feels like something doesn't add up. If He sees it, cares about it, and has the power to stop it then why doesn't He? These are not irreverent questions. In fact, the Psalms are filled with such laments, and Christ Himself echoed them on the cross: "My God, my God, why have you forsaken me?" (*Matthew 27:46*). In this chapter, we begin to explore that "why". It's not necessarily to find complete answers, but to discover how this question can lead us closer to the heart of a God who suffers with us and for us.

2.1
The Unavoidable Question

At some point, everyone who believes in God will ask it:

Why?

Why does a good, loving, all-powerful God allow suffering? Why does He seem to stay silent when our hearts are breaking? Why do children get sick, prayers go unanswered, relationships fall apart, or tragedies strike without warning?

It's a question that feels dangerous to ask but it's one that's always present.

And here's the truth: asking "why" doesn't make you faithless. It makes you human.

The Book of Psalms is filled with cries of pain and confusion. Even King David, called a man after God's own heart, asked in Psalm 13:

"How long, Lord? Will you forget me forever? How long will you hide your face from me?"

These are not words of rebellion. They're words of relationship. A cry from someone who knows God is real but doesn't understand what He's doing.

I've asked this question too. Many times. In fact, there was a time in my life when I became an atheist. Not because I stopped caring about God, but because I couldn't reconcile how an all-loving, all-powerful God could allow so much suffering in the world. The death of innocent children. Calamities that destroy the homes and lives of people who are faithful to Him. It all felt impossible to explain and even harder to accept.

And then there was my sister, Maria Paz. She was a beautiful, loving, and deeply caring mother. The kind of person whose life reflected grace in quiet, consistent ways. She suffered a lot, and yet she was gentle and full of hope. And still… God did not spare her. She died of cervical cancer at a very young age.

I couldn't understand it. I still don't fully. Why her? Why anyone?

But if this question is so unavoidable and if even saints and the Son of God Himself cried it out, then why do so many of us feel guilty for asking it?

Perhaps it's because we've been taught, subtly or overtly, that real faith means having unwavering confidence, an unshakable smile in the face of trial. But the faith of the Church is not blind optimism. It is trust forged in the fire of mystery. Saints like Teresa of Calcutta, John of the Cross, and Thérèse of Lisieux all walked through long, dark nights of the soul. They, too, asked "why" in their own way. And yet they held on, not because they had all the answers, but because they refused to let go of the One who did.

Pain raises the question of God's goodness not because we doubt His existence, but because we expect more from Him. And that expectation, however painful, is actually born of faith. We cry out because we *believe* there is Someone who hears. We lament because deep inside, we know things should be different.

And this is where Christian hope takes root, not in a denial of pain, but in its confrontation. The Catechism of the Catholic Church reminds us that *"Illness and suffering have always been among the gravest problems confronted in human life. In illness, man experiences his powerlessness, his limitations, and his finitude"* (CCC 1500). Yet the Church also teaches that through suffering, *"man discovers his true self, his solidarity with others, and his utter dependence on God."*

So, when we ask *"why,"* we're not betraying God but we are drawing nearer to Him in the most honest way we can. Like a child who doesn't understand, we run to the Father not because we've figured Him out, but because there's nowhere else we'd rather go.

These aren't just philosophical puzzles. These are cries of the heart. And if we're honest, this is where so many people's faith is tested. Not in the absence of belief, but in the presence of pain.

But Scripture doesn't shy away from this. And neither should we. Because even Jesus cried out from the Cross, *"My God, my God, why have you forsaken me?"*

That cry echoes in every believer who has ever felt abandoned, unheard, or broken.

This chapter isn't going to give simple answers because there are none. But what we can offer is a lens. A way of seeing. A faith that dares to ask the hard questions without fear, knowing that God is not threatened by our pain.

In fact, He meets us there.

Grace In The Silence

"How long, Lord? Will you forget me forever? How long will you hide your face from me?"

Psalm 13:1

God's people have always asked hard questions. Scripture doesn't hide them. It honors them. Even our deepest doubts can become prayer when we offer them to the One who sees the whole story even when we can't.

2.2
The Mystery of God's Will

It's natural to ask when we suffer or see someone we love in pain, *"Did God want this to happen?"* Or even more hauntingly, *"Why didn't He stop it?"*

To begin answering that, we need to wrestle with a deep mystery: the will of God.

Catholic theology teaches that God has a **perfect will**. What He desires in fullness, which is always good, holy, and life-giving. But in His wisdom, He also allows a **permissive will**, a space where human freedom, sin, and the brokenness of the world are permitted, though not willed by Him directly.

God does not cause evil. He is never the author of suffering. But He does allow it, for now, within a greater plan that often surpasses our understanding.

And yet, this allowance is not passive. God does not sit back coldly while we suffer. Rather, in His mercy, He actively draws close to the wounded. In His providence, He can use even the darkest moments to accomplish something eternally meaningful. That doesn't mean suffering is good in itself. It means God never lets it be meaningless.

This is not an easy truth to accept. Especially when we're the ones in the middle of the pain.

We want a God who prevents all suffering. But such a God would also have to remove all freedom, all human choice and the world would no longer be one of real love, growth, or redemption. It would be controlled, not free.

It's because of this freedom that sin entered the world, in the first place, through the fall of Adam and Eve. That first break in trust and obedience allowed suffering to touch every part of creation. And yet, even in this fallen world, God does not abandon us. He is still at work, even when we don't see how.

I know this not just as an idea but from experience.

During the COVID pandemic, I faced one of the darkest seasons of my life. Not because I contracted the virus, but because everything else around me seemed to fall apart. The death of my sister tore my heart and dried up my spirit. I was fired from the job I loved, twice in just six months. It left me lost, ashamed, and uncertain of who I was.

It affected my marriage in painful ways. I couldn't bear closeness anymore. I didn't want to be touched, even by my wife Riza. I moved into a separate room, isolated myself, and shut down emotionally. I didn't want to talk. I didn't want to be comforted. I just wanted silence.

And yet even in that silence, God was moving.

One of the hardest truths to accept is that God often works in ways we cannot feel or trace. His silence is not absence. His stillness is not apathy. In fact, some of His greatest miracles begin in hiddenness, in tombs, in wombs, in lonely gardens of agony. The cross itself teaches us this: that the greatest act of love in history came through the greatest act of suffering.

He didn't speak in thunder or clarity. But He sent ordinary, kind and faithful people who helped open me up again to the idea that maybe, just maybe, God still had a plan. His ways weren't clear at the time. But something in me began to stir. A slow, cautious trust started to grow.

And little by little, I began to believe again. Not because the pain disappeared, but because God was gently holding me through it.

This is the essence of *redemptive suffering*. When we unite our pain with Christ's on the Cross, it becomes more than survival, it becomes a sharing in His saving work. As strange as it sounds, our suffering can have eternal value not because it's pleasant, but because it's joined to love.

St. Paul offers us a glimmer of that same hope when he writes:

"We know that all things work together for good for those who love God, who are called according to His purpose." (*Romans 8:28*)

It's not that everything that happens *is* good. But God can draw good from everything. Even tragedy, even loss, even death.

Like a master artist who can take torn fragments and turn them into something beautiful, God can weave our pain into a greater tapestry that only He fully sees.

One day, perhaps, we'll see it too.

But for now, we walk by trust, not by sight, knowing that even when we can't trace His hand, we can choose to hold on to His heart.

Grace In The Silence

"As the heavens are higher than the earth, so are my ways higher than your ways and my thoughts than your thoughts."

Isaiah 55:9

    We don't always understand God's timing or His silence. But we are invited to trust, not because everything makes sense, but because the One who holds our story is good, even when life is not.

2.3
Jesus Didn't Answer It, He Entered It

We often look for answers. But Christianity gives us something even deeper: **a Person**.

When Jesus came into the world, He didn't offer a grand explanation for the problem of suffering. He didn't write a book on why bad things happen to good people. He didn't sit His disciples down and teach a neat philosophical lecture on pain.

Instead, He stepped into it.

Jesus didn't remain at a distance from our sorrow. He took it upon Himself. He wept at the tomb of His friend. He felt the sting of betrayal. He endured sleepless nights, exhaustion, hunger, rejection, mockery, and unimaginable pain. He was misunderstood by His own people and abandoned by His closest friends.

And at the height of it all, He was crucified in the most humiliating and excruciating death known at the time.

He could have avoided it. He could have called down angels, stopped the whole thing, or simply never come in the first place. But He didn't.

Why?

Because the only way to redeem suffering was to enter it.

He didn't just walk into suffering as an act of sympathy. He entered it as a Saviour. Jesus bore the weight of every wound, every sin, every grief, not only to comfort us, but to conquer what separates us from the Father. The

Cross wasn't a tragic accident; it was a chosen path. And in choosing it, He transformed the meaning of pain forever.

By becoming a man, Jesus joined Himself to every human experience including pain. By dying on the Cross, He gave suffering a new meaning. And by rising from the dead, He showed us that pain is not the final word.

This is what makes Christianity so different from any other faith: we worship a God **with scars**.

We don't always get the "why," but we do get the "who."

And in that "who," we discover something remarkable: God's love is not abstract or detached. It bleeds. It cries. It stretches out its arms on a cross and says, "You are not alone." This is the heart of the Gospel. Not that suffering disappears, but that it has been entered, embraced, and ultimately overcome by Love itself

And that changes everything.

When we suffer, we can know with certainty that God is not watching from a distance. He is Emmanuel. God with us. Not just in joy, but in agony. Not just in blessing, but in the wilderness. He meets us in the lowest places of our humanity and fills them with His presence.

So maybe the real comfort doesn't come from a clean answer, but from a pierced hand reaching toward us in the dark.

And for me, this awareness changes the way I approach the Mass. At the Mass, heaven touches earth. The same sacrifice of Calvary is made present. Not repeated, but re-presented for us to enter into. Every time the priest says, *"This is my body, given up for you,"* we are being drawn into that mystery of love and suffering that once happened on the Cross, but now lives eternally in the heart of the Church.

If we truly grasp even a glimpse of what Jesus went through. On how He willingly gave up His life for our salvation, then the Holy Eucharist will never be the same. Every time the priest raises the Body and Blood of Christ, a part of me trembles. Sometimes I feel ashamed... even unworthy to behold something so holy.

It's not guilt. It's awe. It's the quiet realisation that Jesus didn't just suffer *in general* but He suffered *for me*.

And in that moment, I am reminded: the God who suffered still gives Himself to me daily, completely, in love. He enters not only the cross of history but the altar of today. And in receiving Him, I receive the strength to carry my own cross, with Him beside me.

Grace In The Silence

"Surely he has borne our griefs and carried our sorrows... He was pierced for our transgressions, crushed for our iniquities; upon him was the punishment that made us whole, and by his wounds we are healed."

Isaiah 53:4–5

    Jesus didn't stay away from suffering. He took it into His own body. Because of that, our pain is no longer empty. It is known, it is shared, and it can be redeemed.

2.4
Saints Who Suffered Well

We often place the saints on pedestals, imagining they lived lives of peace, power, or miraculous perfection. But the truth is far more real and far more encouraging.

Many of the saints we admire most were no strangers to pain. They didn't just talk about redemptive suffering. They lived it. And they didn't suffer with gritted teeth. Instead, they suffered with open hearts, offering their pain as a prayer. They understood that suffering could become a hidden altar, where love meets sacrifice. And through their lives, we see that holiness isn't found in escaping suffering, but in how we respond to it.

Take **St. Thérèse of Lisieux**, the "Little Flower." She died at just 24 from tuberculosis after years of physical pain and spiritual dryness. Yet she offered every little discomfort even the tiniest acts of sacrifice with love, believing that nothing given to God was ever wasted. She once said, *"Everything is grace."* Even suffering.

Or **St. John Paul II**, who endured the trauma of war, the loss of his family, an assassination attempt, and the slow deterioration of Parkinson's disease. And yet, his papacy became a radiant witness of hope. His suffering did not weaken his ministry. Instead, it magnified it.

St. Teresa of Calcutta, beloved around the world for her service to the poor, spent decades in what she described as a "dark night of the soul," where she could no longer feel the presence of God. Still, she never stopped serving. Her life teaches us that faithfulness does not always feel good but it is a choice made in love.

And **St. Ignatius of Loyola**, a former soldier, found his calling only after being seriously wounded in battle. During his long recovery, he read the lives of the saints and began to desire something greater than earthly glory. That wound changed the direction of his life and through it, the Society of Jesus was born.

These saints didn't "get through" suffering as if it were a detour. They walked straight into it with Christ, and in doing so, discovered its hidden power. Their lives teach us that suffering, when embraced with faith, becomes transformative. Not because it disappears, but because God enters it.

These saints remind us that suffering isn't a sign of failure or punishment. In fact, it's often the soil in which true holiness grows.

You don't have to be a canonised saint to suffer well. I've seen people around me, ordinary believers, walk through painful seasons with quiet trust and radiant faith. Some never complain. Some keep showing up to Mass, holding their pain in silence before the altar. Some continue to give and serve, even when their hearts are heavy.

They may not see themselves as saints. But heaven might disagree.

The Church teaches that all the baptised are called to holiness. Not just the mystics or miracle-workers, but mothers, carpenters, nurses, teachers, the grieving, the lonely, the quietly faithful. In their own way, each is invited to carry the Cross. And in doing so, become a light to others.

In a world that often equates blessing with comfort and success, their witness flips the script. They show us that holiness doesn't always wear a smile but it always clings to hope.

Their lives become a kind of living gospel and a proof that Christ is real and grace is possible.

And maybe, in our own suffering, we are being invited to join that communion. To become living witnesses of love, even when life hurts. And when we struggle to carry that cross, we can look to the saints not as unreachable icons, but as companions who walked this road before us. And who are now cheering us on.

Grace In The Silence

"We rejoice in our sufferings, knowing that suffering produces endurance, and endurance produces character, and character produces hope."

Romans 5:3–4

The saints didn't rejoice in pain itself, but in what God could do through it. Suffering, when united with Christ, doesn't end in despair. It deepens endurance. Shapes character. And leads us, always, to hope.

2.5
Faith Doesn't Eliminate the Question But It Changes the Journey

By now, you may realise something important: faith doesn't give us all the answers. It doesn't erase every doubt. It doesn't explain every loss.

But it changes how we live with the questions.

It doesn't tidy them up. It doesn't always quiet them down. But it gives them context. It anchors the cry in a relationship. It reminds us that we're not shouting into a void but we're speaking to a Father.

To believe in God, especially in the face of pain, isn't about pretending everything is okay. It's about choosing to trust someone bigger than the pain. It's about saying, "*I don't understand this but I know You are with me.*"

And that changes everything.

It's easy to think that strong faith means never asking "why." But the Bible tells a different story. Job asked. David asked. The prophets asked. Even Jesus asked.

If the Son of God could cry out in anguish and still entrust Himself to the Father, then there's room for our sorrow and faith to coexist too. He shows us that questioning isn't the opposite of belief, it's often the doorway into deeper intimacy.

What faith offers is not a quick fix but a deeper presence. A quiet strength. A peace that doesn't come from having everything figured out, but from knowing we are not alone.

Faith gives us room to grieve honestly, but not without hope. It teaches us that tears are not a sign of weakness, and silence is not a sign of God's absence. Often, God speaks most powerfully in the quiet moments, in the stillness, in the Eucharist, in the kindness of a friend, in the Word that comes at just the right time.

He is present in the sacraments, where grace touches us not just spiritually, but physically. In Confession, we receive mercy. In the Eucharist, we receive Christ Himself, Body, Blood, Soul, and Divinity. These are not just rituals. They are encounters. God meets us in the midst of our weakness, and whispers: *"I am here."*

Faith is not a straight line. It's a pilgrimage. Like the disciples on the road to Emmaus, we often walk in sorrow, not recognising that Christ walks beside us. But He does. And in time, like them, our hearts begin to burn with a new understanding, not always of answers, but of His presence.

It doesn't mean the road ahead will be easy. But faith means we walk it with Someone who has already walked it first.

I've come to realise that the goal isn't to stop asking "why." It's to learn how to walk forward even while the question remains.

To hold pain in one hand and trust in the other.

To keep showing up.

To keep listening.

To keep holding on.

The question of *why* has echoed through every heart that has known pain: Why would a good and loving God allow suffering? While the answer is never simple, faith gives us a way to carry the question with courage.

God does not cause suffering. In His mysterious will, He allows it in a world shaped by sin and freedom. And instead of staying distant, He entered our pain through the person of Jesus. His suffering doesn't explain ours but it redeems it.

The saints didn't escape suffering, and neither do we. But they teach us that even our wounds can become places where grace flows.

Faith doesn't erase pain or answer every question. It simply changes the journey from walking alone to walking with the One who carries us.

And we don't walk this road alone. God gives us the Church not just as an institution, but as a family of fellow travellers. Saints above, and companions beside us, who help carry the burden when it feels too heavy to bear alone.

We may still ask "why." But now we ask it in relationship with trust that, even in darkness, God is working for good.

And so we press on not in certainty, but in surrender.

Not because we've resolved every question, but because we've entrusted them to the One who holds us. Faith does not silence the "why" but it teaches us to live faithfully while it remains unanswered, and to believe that one day, perhaps in eternity, it will give way to joy.

Grace In The Silence

"Father, if you are willing, take this cup away from me; yet not my will, but yours be done."

Luke 22:42

Even Jesus asked for another way. And yet, in love, He surrendered. This is not weakness. Instead, it's the strongest prayer of trust ever spoken. It shows us that faith doesn't mean avoiding the cross, but embracing it because we know what comes after.

CHAPTER 3

NO OTHER WAY BUT PAIN

Pain is not just something we survive but it can be something we grow through. While God does not take pleasure in our suffering, He allows it as a means for purification, transformation, and communion with Christ. There are depths in the human heart and soul that can only be reached through the Cross.

Suffering, when embraced with faith, becomes more than a burden. It becomes a path. In our pain, we are invited to journey more deeply into the mystery of Christ's Passion. Just as Jesus' suffering was not in vain, ours too can bear fruit when united with His. The Catholic understanding of redemptive suffering teaches us that our trials, offered in love, can become a source of grace for ourselves and for others.

There are no shortcuts in the Christian journey. Holiness is forged in the fire of affliction, not in comfort or ease. While we naturally resist pain, it is often in those very moments of weakness and breaking that God's strength shines through. In choosing to walk the way of the Cross, we are not choosing defeat, we are choosing to be conformed to Christ, who suffered, died, and rose again so that our suffering might have eternal meaning.

3.1
The Lie Of Comfort Culture

We live in a world that does everything it can to avoid pain.

Just look around. You'll see painkillers that you can imagine for every physical ache, entertainment for every boredom, noise to drown out the silence. We're constantly told that comfort is the highest good and suffering is a problem to solve, not something to sit with or learn from.

This culture trains us to believe that if we're hurting, something must be wrong. That if life isn't smooth, we must have failed. That happiness is found in avoiding discomfort, inconvenience, or anything that makes us feel weak or broken.

But Scripture and the lives of the saints would tell a very different story.

They show us that pain isn't always the enemy. That sometimes, it's the only road to something deeper. That God doesn't always remove our suffering but He never wastes it.

The world says: avoid pain at all costs.

But Jesus says: *"Take up your cross and follow me."* (*Matthew 16:24*)

Those are not the words of a motivational speaker. They're the call of a Saviour who knows that real love always costs something.

The danger with comfort culture is not comfort itself, but what it does to the soul when it becomes our highest aim. It makes us allergic to anything that stretches us. It makes holiness look unreasonable. It makes the Cross seem offensive. And slowly, without even realising it, we begin to believe that a life worth living is a life without sacrifice.

If we build our lives around the pursuit of comfort, we'll end up with a shallow faith. One that falls apart when real hardship comes. One that treats God like a vending machine or an insurance policy rather than a Father who invites us to trust Him, even when it hurts.

The comfort culture teaches us that suffering is meaningless. But the Catholic faith teaches us the opposite: suffering, united with Christ, becomes a powerful act of love. It becomes redemptive not just for ourselves, but for the Church and the world.

Comfort, in itself, isn't bad. But when it becomes our goal, it can blind us to what God is doing in the pain we're trying to avoid. We miss the grace hidden in the struggle. We miss the nearness of Christ who suffers with us and through us.

There's a reason the saints didn't chase pleasure, popularity, or safety. They chased Christ. And more often than not, that road led through suffering.

Because the Cross is not just a one-time event. It's a way of life for every disciple.

The world teaches us to run from the Cross.

The Gospel teaches us to carry it with Christ, and because of Christ.

And strangely, that path, the one we try so hard to avoid, is the only one that leads to real joy. Not the fleeting kind the world offers, but the deep, unshakable joy that comes from knowing we are becoming who we were made to be: holy, free, and full of love.

Grace In The Silence

"Enter through the narrow gate. For wide is the gate and broad is the road that leads to destruction, and many enter through it. But small is the gate and narrow the road that leads to life, and only a few find it."

Matthew 7:13–14

    The wide road is easy. It avoids pain. But it also leads nowhere. The narrow road is hard and yet it leads to life. Not just after death, but now. Right here, even in the middle of suffering, God is shaping something eternal in us.

3.2
Pain as the Furnace of Growth

Growth doesn't happen in ease. It happens in tension, in fire, in struggle.

Just like gold is refined in fire, and muscles are built through strain, our souls are shaped in the furnace of suffering. Not because pain is good in itself but because it reveals, purifies, and strengthens what nothing else can reach.

It's not a comfortable truth. But it's a deeply biblical one.

Jesus said, *"Every branch that does bear fruit he prunes so that it will be even more fruitful."* (John 15:2)

Pruning is painful. It involves cutting. But it's not punishment. It's love with a vision. God doesn't cut us down. He cuts us *back*, so we can grow stronger, deeper, and more alive in Him.

Suffering has a way of bringing hidden things to the surface. It exposes the motives behind our service, the cracks in our character, and the unspoken expectations we place on God and others. And that exposure, while painful, is often the first step toward real transformation.

Some of the most beautiful virtues like patience, humility, forgiveness, compassion, are almost impossible to learn without suffering. Pain softens our pride. It sharpens our empathy. It teaches us how to rely on God, not just in theory, but in the gritty reality of everyday life.

I've seen this truth in my own life especially in my journey of service within Couples For Christ.

Before we were discerned to become Cluster Heads of the South Chapter, which was still a chapter back then, I went through one of the most painful ministry seasons I've ever experienced. I faced conflict, not just with people outside the community, but with fellow leaders and members I was serving closely with.

I felt rejected, misunderstood, and deeply disrespected. It was heart-breaking, because I had given so much. I made sacrifices, poured my time and energy into service, and yet I felt like all of it was for nothing.

At one point, I was even humiliated publicly. That moment shattered my focus. I allowed anger and resentment to grow in my heart instead of fighting for the relationships I once cherished.

But now, looking back as a Cluster Leader, I can see it differently.

That season wasn't pointless. It was God refining me. He was allowing the fire, not to burn me down, but to build me up. To remove my pride. To deepen my compassion. To prepare me for a kind of

leadership that isn't based on recognition, but on faithfulness and humility.

He was teaching me that ministry is not about being liked, but about being Christ-like.

He was stripping away the need for approval so that I could serve with freer hands and a quieter heart.

I'm still a work in progress. But I have grown. So much. Spiritually, emotionally, and pastorally. That pain, though I never would have chosen it, made me a better servant of His.

And that's the strange gift of suffering: we rarely understand it in the moment, but we often see its fruit in the aftermath.

Pain forces us to confront what we really believe in about God, about others, and about ourselves.

And if we let it, it can deepen our roots in Christ. It can turn shallow faith into real conviction. It can turn wounds into wisdom. And most of all, it can make us more like Jesus, the Man of Sorrows, who was no stranger to grief, but who trusted the Father through it all.

Grace In The Silence

"In this you rejoice, although now for a little while you may have to suffer through various trials, so that the genuineness of your faith, more precious than gold that is perishable even though tested by fire, may prove to be for praise, glory, and honour at the revelation of Jesus Christ."

1 Peter 1:6–7

Faith that's never tested may shine for a while. But faith that has passed through fire? That kind of faith lasts. It honours God not just in words but in endurance, in trust, in surrender.

3.3
The Cross Is Not Optional And Our Mother Knows The Way

Cross isn't a metaphor. It is real.

And it pierces us where we love most.

We often love the idea of following Jesus. The teachings, the miracles, the peace, the promise of heaven, they all draw us in. But many of us, myself included, have struggled with this part:

"Whoever wants to be my disciple must deny themselves, take up their cross daily, and follow me."

Luke 9:23

This isn't a poetic line meant for Holy Week reflections. This is the heart of the Christian life.

To follow Jesus means we cannot avoid the Cross.

This might sound harsh especially in a world that avoids suffering at all costs. But Jesus wasn't calling us to masochism or spiritual misery. He was calling us to a deeper freedom. The kind that only comes when we stop clinging to our comfort, our ego, or even our own understanding.

The Cross is not just the place where Jesus died but it's the path He walked. And it's the one He invites us to walk with Him.

For a long time, I thought carrying the cross meant dealing with hardship passively and just tolerating suffering while trying to stay religious. But I've learned that real discipleship means carrying the cross actively. It means choosing love when resentment feels easier. Choosing humility when I want to defend my pride. Choosing forgiveness when I've been wounded. Choosing trust when everything in me wants to run or shut down.

That's the kind of cross that shows up every day.

And sometimes, it shows up in ways that completely break you.

On November 10, 2023, my only son, Shann, left the house without anyone noticing. It was early dawn, around 3:30 a.m. He was wearing nothing but jogging pants, a shirt, and a bag on a cold, wintery morning. I was asleep in the other room, and Riza was working a night shift.

I didn't wake until 7:30 a.m. when I got up to pick up Riza. As I walked downstairs, I felt how cold the house had become and then I saw the main door wide open. I ran to Shann's room. Empty. I opened every door. Nothing.

My heart sank. I felt the weight of the world press down on me. I checked the CCTV footage and saw it. Shann walking out into the dark, alone.

I froze.

I couldn't think. I couldn't breathe. My tears began to fall uncontrollably. I ran outside, down the road, turning every corner, hoping I might see him, even just a glimpse. Nothing.

I called the police. They came. But I couldn't speak. I literally couldn't find words. They had to call Riza for me and broker her the news.

That moment shattered me. It was the most excruciating pain I've ever felt as a father. And even now, though that moment has passed, I still carry it. Every morning, I feel the ache. Every time I see my son struggle with the pressures of life, with expectations, with the weight the world tries to place on him. I feel it again.

The police found him after eight agonising hours near the motorway, where they believed he was intending to jump and end his life. He was all wet, his jogging pants and shoes caked with mud. When I saw him, I hugged him so tightly, wishing with everything in me that that embrace could somehow pull the pain out of him and into me.

There are pieces of that day I still can't remember. I don't know if it's because my mind is trying to forget, or because my brain simply

couldn't bear the weight of it. The police had checked his bag, but it was only after they'd gone that Riza found something inside, an image of Our Lady of Guadalupe.

At first, I didn't know what to make of it. But the more I sat with that moment, the more I realised that she was there. Always.

She was with him.

In the darkness, in the cold, in his confusion and pain, Our Lady, the Mother of Sorrows, had not abandoned him. She had walked with him, silently, as she once walked with her own Son on the road to Calvary. That image, found in the bag after everything, wasn't just a detail. It was a sign. A reminder that even when we cannot reach the ones we love, Mary is already there, praying, protecting, weeping, and interceding.

Our Lady of Guadalupe is known as the Mother of the Americas, the Patroness of the Unborn, the one who brings consolation to the poor and broken-hearted. She appeared to St. Juan Diego not with thunder and might, but with tenderness. And on that morning, in our own agony, she came again, quietly, hidden in a backpack, bringing with her the presence of God's mercy in a moment we didn't understand.

And perhaps, that is what Mary does best. She enters our suffering not to explain it, but to accompany us through it.

She teaches us how to stand at the foot of the Cross not with bitterness, but with trust. Not with answers, but with love.

In hindsight, I believe she was reminding me that even when I felt completely helpless as a father, she had not let go of my son. And she hadn't let go of me.

This is my cross. It's not a cross I chose. But it's the one I've been asked to carry. Not in anger. Not in despair. But in love and with Christ.

Because the truth is: there is no Christian life without the cross.

There is no spiritual maturity without sacrifice.

There is no resurrection without crucifixion.

And the most hopeful part?

We don't carry it alone.

Jesus doesn't stand at a distance, watching us struggle. He carries it with us. Sometimes, He carries us. That's what makes the Cross redemptive rather than destructive. It becomes a place of communion. Of encounter. Of deep union with Christ.

And through that union, our pain becomes a participation in His redeeming love.

The world will continue to promise a cross-less Christianity. One that offers blessings without cost, comfort without sacrifice, and healing without surrender. But that version of faith is shallow, and when life falls apart, it cannot hold.

The saints knew this. The Church teaches this. The Gospel declares it: the Cross is not a side path. It is **the** path. And strangely, paradoxically, mysteriously, it is also the path to joy. Because when we carry the Cross with Christ, we discover not just His pain, but His presence, His peace, and His power.

He transforms our wounds into wells of grace.

He turns our brokenness into beauty.

And He walks with us, every step of the way until the Cross gives way to the empty tomb.

Grace In The Silence

"Whoever does not take up their cross and follow me is not worthy of me. Whoever finds their life will lose it, and whoever loses their life for my sake will find it."

Matthew 10:38–39

The Cross isn't just a burden, it's the place where we discover what it really means to live. In giving ourselves away, we find ourselves. In dying to self, we find Christ. And in Christ, we find everything.

3.4
There Is No Resurrection Without the Cross

The story of our faith does not end at Calvary.

But it must pass through it.

In a world obsessed with shortcuts and quick fixes, the message of the Cross can feel unbearable. And yet, it's the only path Jesus laid out. He never promised a pain-free life but a resurrected one.

Too often, we want Easter Sunday without Good Friday. We want joy without struggle, glory without sacrifice, victory without battle. But that's not the pattern Christ gave us. His path was descent before ascent. Suffering before healing. Death before life.

There is no resurrection without the cross.

This isn't just poetic language. It's the very shape of redemption. The Paschal Mystery is not just a chapter in the Gospels; it is the pattern of our lives. As Catholics, every Mass brings us face to face with it. In the Eucharist, we encounter both the sacrifice of the Cross and the triumph of the Resurrection held together, never separated.

That truth doesn't make the suffering easier, but it gives it meaning. It tells us that our wounds aren't the end of the story, that when united with Christ, they can become wells of grace.

Jesus' suffering didn't just lead to His resurrection. It made ours possible.

That's why St. Paul could write:

"I want to know Christ, yes, to know the power of his resurrection and participation in his sufferings, becoming like him in his death."

(Philippians 3:10)

It almost sounds strange when you say *participation in His sufferings*? Who would *want* that?

But Paul understood something we often forget: suffering with Christ means rising with Him too. The pain we carry isn't pointless. It's part of a deeper transformation. A dying to ourselves so that we can be raised into something greater.

Sometimes resurrection looks dramatic like healing, or reconciliation, or the lifting of a burden. But other times, it's quiet. It's the ability to keep loving when your heart has been broken. The courage to forgive when you've been wounded. The grace to smile again after a season of sorrow.

These are little resurrections. Signs that new life is still possible. Proof that God is still at work.

And they only come through the Cross.

Even the saints were not spared this path. In fact, they embraced it. St. Thérèse of Lisieux once said, *"Suffering united with love is no longer suffering, but a gift."* They understood what our culture tries to forget: that the way up is often the way down, and that resurrection doesn't erase the wounds, it transfigures them.

I've come to see my own pain differently through this lens. Not as a dead end, but as holy ground. The very place where God does His most mysterious, powerful work, not in spite of suffering, but *through* it.

The cross we carry might leave scars. But they are the kind of scars that speak of resurrection.

They tell the world: *I've been through death… and by God's grace, I live.*

Grace In The Silence

"Unless a grain of wheat falls to the ground and dies, it remains alone. But if it dies, it produces much fruit."

John 12:24

Death is not the end. In Christ, it is the beginning. Every surrender, every loss, every breaking open, when given to Him, becomes a seed. And from that seed, life can grow.

3.5
When We Don't Feel Strong Enough

Everything we've said about pain and the Cross is true. But it's also hard.

And maybe, right now, you're reading all of this and thinking:

That sounds beautiful… but I just don't think I have the strength for it.

You're not alone.

There have been many times in my own life when I've felt exactly that. Times when I've looked at my situation, my exhaustion, or my inner turmoil and thought, *Lord, I can't do this. I'm not strong enough.*

here have been many times in my own life when I've felt exactly that. Times when I've looked at my situation, my exhaustion, or my inner turmoil and thought, *Lord, I can't do this. I'm not strong enough.*

One of the clearest moments was when my son, Shann, disappeared one rainy morning. Those eight hours felt like a lifetime. I wasn't just terrified, I was paralysed. I couldn't think, couldn't speak. It was as though all strength had left my body. I remember running through the streets, searching desperately, crying out to God with no words, only pain.

Even now, that day lingers. The weight of it hasn't vanished. There are mornings I still wake up and feel it all over again. In those moments, I've had to face the truth: I don't have the strength for this. Not on my own.

And I believe that's the most honest place to begin.

Because here's the good news: you're not expected to be strong enough.

God never asked you to carry your cross alone or to carry it perfectly.

He only asked you to say yes.

In 2 Corinthians 12, when Paul begged God to take away his suffering, the Lord responded not with a solution, but with a promise:

"My grace is sufficient for you, for my power is made perfect in weakness." , 2 Corinthians 12:9

That verse has carried me through more seasons than I can count. Not because it removed the pain, but because it reminded me that I don't need to have it all together to walk with Christ. I just need to show up. To say "yes" again. Even when it's trembling. Even when it's whispered through tears.

Our weakness isn't an obstacle to God. It's often where He works best.

We forget that even Jesus, in His humanity, reached a moment when He felt the weight of the Cross before it even touched His shoulders. In Gethsemane, He said, "My soul is sorrowful, even to the point of death." He sweat blood. He asked, if possible, to let the cup pass. But in His weakness, He didn't run. He leaned into the Father. And in that leaning, He found the strength to say, *"Not my will, but yours be done."*

That same grace is offered to us.

Some days, your "yes" might be bold and joyful. Other days, it might be a quiet decision to just get out of bed, to pray a simple prayer, or to take one small step forward. That counts. In the Kingdom of God, even the smallest act of faith becomes a flame that cannot be extinguished.

Sacramentally, too, God meets us in our weakness. In Confession, He lifts us. In the Eucharist, He feeds us. In every Mass, He gives us the very strength we lack. Not symbolically, but really. His grace is not abstract but it is poured out, embodied, and present in the sacraments for moments exactly like these.

Remember: the saints we admire didn't make it through life because they were superhuman. They made it because they kept going. They kept trusting. They fell, but they kept returning to the Father.

And you can too.

Whatever cross you're carrying, however heavy it feels, God is not asking you to lift it with superhuman strength. He's asking you to lean into His. He's asking you to trust that *He* is strong enough.

And that is more than enough.

We long for healing, growth, and resurrection but the way to all of these often passes through suffering.

This chapter reminded us that in a world obsessed with comfort, the Gospel calls us to carry the Cross. Not as a burden to fear, but as a sacred path that leads to transformation. Pain is not meaningless. In God's hands, it becomes the furnace where faith is purified, character is shaped, and love is deepened.

We looked at how our pain, like the pruning of a fruitful vine, is often God's way of preparing us for greater things. We cannot skip the Cross and still hope to share in the Resurrection. There is no shortcut to holiness.

But we are never asked to walk this road alone. When we don't feel strong enough, Christ walks with us. When we fall, His grace holds us. And every tear we shed, every wound we carry, becomes a place where He can meet us and make us new.

So if the road you're on is painful, don't assume you've gone the wrong way.

You may be walking the very path Jesus walked first.

And that path always leads to life.

Grace In The Silence

"Come to me, all you who are weary and burdened, and I will give you rest. Take my yoke upon you and learn from me… For my yoke is easy, and my burden is light."

Matthew 11:28–30

    Jesus never said you had to carry it alone. When the weight is too much, He invites you to walk beside Him, to share the burden. And with every step, He promises: *You are not alone. I am with you.*

CHAPTER 4
OVERCOMING PAIN

Pain is inevitable in life. Whether physical, emotional, or spiritual, we all encounter suffering in one form or another. But while pain can often feel overwhelming, it doesn't have to define us.

As Christians, we are not promised a life free from suffering. Christ Himself embraced pain, bearing the weight of the Cross and inviting us to take up our own. Yet He did not suffer without purpose. His wounds became the wellspring of our healing, His death the path to new life. In our own suffering, we are drawn into a mysterious participation in His redemptive love. Overcoming pain, then, is not about denying our struggles but learning to unite them with His.

This chapter will offer both spiritual insight and practical guidance on how we can navigate seasons of pain with faith and hope. We'll look at the importance of prayer, community, acceptance, and meaning-making. More than survival, the aim is transformation. A heart made stronger, more compassionate, and more rooted in Christ. Pain may scar us, but it need not break us. Through grace, it can even sanctify us.

4.1
Start Where You Are

When you're in pain, the last thing you need is someone telling you to "*be strong*" or "*have more faith.*" Pain isn't a problem to be solved quickly. It's an ache that touches the core of our humanity. In the thick of it, even the simplest acts like getting out of bed, making it through the day, or just breathing, can feel monumental. Sometimes, prayer becomes a struggle. The words won't come. The silence feels heavy. And if we're honest, there are moments we wonder if God is even listening.

The truth is, when you're suffering, even getting out of bed can feel like a small miracle. Sometimes, prayer feels impossible. Sometimes, you don't know what to say to God or if you even want to say anything at all.

And that's okay.

Because healing doesn't begin with perfection. Instead, it begins with honesty.

One of the greatest lies we can believe is that we have to get ourselves together before we come to God. That we need to feel more faith, pray more eloquently, or somehow prove that we're worthy of healing.

But the Gospel tells a different story.

In the Gospels, the people Jesus responded to most tenderly weren't those with polished words or strong spiritual résumés. They were the ones who simply came, messy, broken, exhausted, desperate. The bleeding woman who reached out just to touch His cloak. The blind man who wouldn't stop shouting. The father who cried out, *"I believe, help my unbelief!"* (Mark 9:24)

That's all it takes: showing up.

I've learned this firsthand in the hardest seasons of my life when grief, confusion, or depression made it hard to even think about prayer. There were times when all I could do was whisper, "Lord, I'm here. I don't know what to say. I just need You."

I remember one particular season during my time serving in the community, when everything around me looked fruitful on the outside. Events were running, talks were being given, people were blessed. But inside, I was quietly falling apart. I was overwhelmed, spiritually dry, and silently battling anxiety I couldn't explain. I still showed up to serve, but each meeting, each talk, felt heavier than the last. I couldn't bring myself to pray the way I used to; even lifting my hands in worship felt hollow. And yet, in that silence, God didn't withdraw. He waited. There was no lightning bolt moment, but little by little, I began to feel seen again. Not because I had figured everything out, but because I stopped pretending and let Him meet me where I actually was.

And somehow… that was enough.

Because God is not looking for performance. He's looking for hearts.

He meets us where we are, not where we wish we were. His grace flows not into our strength, but into our weakness.

So if today, all you can do is cry. Do that.

If all you can offer is silence. Offer it.

If all you can say is, "Help me". Say it.

Start where you are.

Because that's exactly where Christ wants to meet you.

The saints remind us that progress in the spiritual life is often slow, hidden, and full of setbacks. St. Thérèse of Lisieux spoke of her "little way", a path of trusting God's mercy in her littleness. Her example is a reminder that even the smallest act of turning toward God, especially in our pain, is precious to Him. We don't need to have grand gestures or lofty prayers. Sometimes the most powerful prayer is the most fragile one: "Lord, I can't do this without You."

And here's something worth holding onto: starting where you are doesn't mean staying where you are. God is a Father who welcomes us as we are, but loves us too much to leave us there. As we open our hearts to Him, even in the smallest, most broken ways, His grace begins to do what we cannot. It's not about willing ourselves to get better or forcing our faith to grow overnight. It's about trusting that the One who began the work in us will bring it to completion (cf. Philippians 1:6).

There is comfort in knowing we don't journey alone. We are part of the Body of Christ, and the Church offers us not only the Sacraments but also the communion of saints, those in heaven who intercede for us, and those around us who walk with us. When we cannot pray, the Church prays with and for us. When we cannot believe, we can lean on the faith of others. This is the grace of community. This is the strength of belonging to something greater than ourselves.

Grace In The Silence

"Come to me, all you who are weary and burdened, and I will give you rest."

Matthew 11:28

God doesn't wait for you to be ready. He calls you in your weariness, in your burden, in your mess. His invitation is not to the perfect, but to the broken who are willing to come.

4.2
The Power of Prayer When It's Hard to Pray

There are seasons when prayer flows easily, when we feel God's nearness and words come freely.

And then there are the other seasons. The ones where silence stretches like an empty hallway. Where prayer feels dry, repetitive, or even pointless. Where we wonder if God is even listening. If you're in that place, you are not alone.

Many saints, men and women of deep prayer, walked through these same dry and desolate seasons. St. Teresa of Calcutta lived for years in what she called *"the darkness,"* feeling no spiritual consolation. And yet, she remained faithful. Why? Because prayer is not about feeling. It's about relationship**.** It's not always about words. Sometimes, it's simply showing up.

When you're in pain, prayer often becomes less about saying the right things and more about just being with God in the rawness of your soul. Sometimes the most honest prayer is silence. Sometimes it's just, *"Lord, I'm tired,"* or *"Lord, I don't even know what to pray."*

And that's okay.

There were countless moments in my life when prayer felt like too much of a hassle.

I'd rather watch Netflix. Or go out for a drink. Anything but face that quiet space with God. Deep down, I knew I needed prayer. I even bought books, hoping they'd help me get started. But they just ended up collecting dust on a shelf like the rest.

I wasn't lazy. I was just tired. Spiritually dry. Unmotivated. And a little lost.

What surprised me, though, was how music began to draw me back to God, slowly, gently. I became emotional when I listened to Christian songs I could relate to. They expressed what I couldn't put into words. And little by little, music became my prayer, my way back into God's presence.

It didn't look "religious" at first. But it was real. And God met me there.

Here are a few ways to stay connected in prayer even when it's hard:

1. Pray the Psalms

The Book of Psalms is full of raw, emotional, sometimes even angry prayers. They teach us that there is no emotion too big or too messy for God. If you don't have your own words, borrow David's.

Try reading Psalm 6, Psalm 13, or Psalm 42. Read slowly. Let them become your own.

2. Cling to the Rosary

The Rosary is a gift in times of suffering. When your heart is numb or heavy, letting the rhythm of Hail Marys guide you becomes a kind of spiritual breathing. Even if you don't feel anything, keep going. Mary knows pain. She will pray with you.

And if you can, sit before the Blessed Sacrament, even if just for a few minutes. There were times I went to Adoration and said nothing at all. I just sat there, tired and unsure of what I was even doing. But something shifted in that stillness. Not outwardly, but quietly, inside me. Just being in the presence of Jesus, body, blood, soul, and divinity, reminded me that I was not alone. Sometimes, His silent presence speaks more than a thousand words ever could.

3. Listen to Your Favourite Christian Songs

Sometimes music reaches the soul when spoken prayer cannot. Put on songs that remind you of God's love and truth, even if you don't feel like singing along. Let the lyrics become your prayer.

I remember a prayer assembly I attended during one of the toughest points in my ministry. I was drained, burned out, and honestly didn't feel like being there. But as others began to sing and pray around me, I just closed my eyes and let their voices carry me. I didn't say anything aloud. I couldn't. But something in my spirit softened. That day, their prayer became mine. And I learned something: when we can't pray for ourselves, community can carry us.

Whether it's Casting Crowns, Liveloud or a simple worship playlist, music has a way of carrying our hearts back to God. You may cry. You may simply sit and let it wash over you. That *is* prayer, too.

4. Offer Small Prayers Throughout the Day

Sometimes the long prayers are too much. That's okay. Offer small, sincere moments to God:

- *"Jesus, I trust in You."*
- *"Stay with me, Lord."*
- *"Be my strength."*
- *"Help me breathe."*

God hears them all.

Even Jesus, in the Garden of Gethsemane, experienced agony in prayer. He sweat blood. He cried out,

"Father, if You are willing, take this cup from Me" (Luke 22:42). That prayer wasn't polished, it was painful. But He still prayed. He still turned to the Father. When our prayers are soaked in weariness or fear, we're not far from Christ, we're sharing in His moment of greatest vulnerability.

5. Let Others Pray for You

There are times when you can't carry your own prayer and that's why the Church is a body. Ask others to pray for you. Let their faith uphold you. Even if you feel empty, you are still held in the prayers of the saints and the Church.

I've had days when my prayer was nothing but tears.

Days when the Rosary felt like just words.

Days when I sat in silence and said nothing at all.

Sometimes, it was only a worship song that could help me lift my eyes again.

But somehow, even in that emptiness, something holy was happening.

Because prayer isn't about performance. It's about being there..

Just show up.

Prayer, at its core, is not just about saying things to God. It's about being *with* Him. Whether through tears, music, silence, or the gentle repetition of a Rosary bead, what matters most is the heart that seeks Him. Even when we don't feel it, even when heaven seems quiet, every effort to turn toward God is met with His gaze. He never turns away.

Grace In The Silence

"In the same way, the Spirit helps us in our weakness. For we do not know how to pray as we ought, but the Spirit himself intercedes for us with sighs too deep for words."

Romans 8:26

Even when you can't pray, the Holy Spirit prays in you. Your sighs, your silence, your tears, and yes, even your songs, are heard. And they are enough.

4.3
Anchored in the Sacraments

When we are overwhelmed by suffering, we instinctively search for something steady, something real. The sacraments are not just rituals or obligations of faith. They are lifelines. They are God's concrete and consistent ways of pouring grace into our wounded hearts, often when we need it most.

In particular, the Holy Eucharist holds a special place in my journey. It was the turning point that brought me back to the very faith I once rejected.

Back in the year 2000, I found myself in the deepest confusion of my Christian life. What began as honest questioning eventually turned into bitterness. I walked away from the seminary, turned my back on the Church, and declared myself an atheist. I went from being a man of faith to someone who actively tried to dismantle it. I debated believers in the streets, openly attacked the Church, and felt a sense of disgust even at the mention of God. My heart became hardened, and I thought I had found strength in that rebellion.

Then in 2004, I married Riza, one of the most faithful women I know. It was through her gentle, unwavering witness that cracks slowly began to appear in my hardened heart. I went to Mass with her, but I

kept my distance emotionally and spiritually. I still carried all that anger inside me. I even joined Freemasonry, looking for meaning and belonging outside the Church, and for a while, it seemed like I had found it.

But God wasn't finished with me.

In 2013, Riza was invited to a Christian Life Program (CLP) hosted by Couples for Christ in Cardiff. I went with her, not because I wanted to, but because I didn't want to disappoint her. What I thought would be a quick weekend of talks turned into an encounter that shook the foundation of everything I thought I believed.

At first, I resisted. I showed up in a suit, distanced myself, and filled my mind with criticisms. But during the pray-over session, something unexpected happened. As the team prayed over me and Fr. Gareth laid his hand on my shoulder, I felt something break inside me. My tears flowed uncontrollably. I wasn't even sure what was happening, but I knew something holy was taking place.

And then we went to Mass.

I expected bitterness. I expected the same old internal resistance. But as soon as I entered the church, I felt something I hadn't felt in years, peace. A deep, unexplainable peace. It was as if the Lord Himself whispered, *"You're home."*

Suddenly, everything about the Mass made sense. The words weren't just words. The gestures weren't empty routines. And when the priest raised the chalice and said, *"This is the chalice of my blood... poured out for you and for many..."*, something within me shattered again. For the first time, the Eucharist became real. It wasn't just theology. It was personal. It was love. It was Jesus giving Himself for me, even when I had given up on Him.

Alongside the Eucharist, the Sacrament of Reconciliation became a wellspring of grace in my return journey. After years of rejecting God, going to confession was intimidating, almost terrifying. I felt exposed, ashamed, and unsure of what I would even say. But what I encountered wasn't judgement. It was mercy. Through the priest, Christ met me with tenderness, not condemnation. The words of absolution felt like healing balm over years of spiritual wounds. It reminded me that the sacraments are not rewards for the good, they are medicine for the broken.

That moment became a defining point in my life. It became the anchor I return to when I'm struggling, when I'm lost, or when I feel unworthy. It reminds me that God never gave up on me, and that He still meets me in every Eucharist, offering Himself fully.

Not long after, Riza and I decided to make things right. Though we were already married civilly, we hadn't yet been sacramentally married in the Church. In 2014, we stood before God, now with open hearts, and received the sacrament of marriage. And beautifully, it was Fr. Gareth, who had been part of my turning point, who officiated and blessed our union.

Looking back, I realise now that in each sacrament I had received, baptism, reconciliation, the Eucharist, and marriage, Christ wasn't waiting for my perfection. He was stepping into my imperfection with grace. This is the power of the sacraments: they are not just human rituals, but divine encounters. When we approach them with honesty, even if we feel unworthy, Jesus meets us there. He doesn't shy away from our mess. He enters it, just as He entered the world through a manger and climbed a Cross for our salvation.

That experience reminds me that the sacraments are not just for the pious or the perfect. They are for the wounded, the skeptical, the lost, and the angry. They are for those who don't know how to come back. And through them, God says, *"Come as you are."*

The Eucharist became the moment I came home, but it also became the place I keep returning to, again and again. Because in every season of pain, confusion, or weakness, I know this much: Christ is there, fully present, fully given. And that is more than enough to begin again.

This is what I hold onto when life hurts or when my faith feels thin. The sacraments aren't just moments from the past but they are anchors I still cling to today. They sustain me when prayer is dry, when pain runs deep, and when I need to remember who I am and whose I am. Every time I receive the Eucharist, every time I enter the confessional, every time I bless myself with holy water, I'm reminded: grace is still flowing. Healing is still possible. And Christ is still drawing near.

Grace In The Silence

"This is my body, which is given for you. Do this in remembrance of me."

Luke 22:19

In the Eucharist, Jesus does not simply remind us of His love, He makes it present. And every time we receive Him, we are reminded that grace is not earned. It is offered freely, especially when we least deserve it.

4.4
Let People In

Pain has a way of isolating us.

When we're hurting, physically, emotionally, or spiritually, our instinct is often to withdraw. We hide, we shrink, we protect. We fear being misunderstood, judged, or worse, seen as weak. So we put on a brave face. We smile when we're breaking inside. And we tell ourselves,

"No one will understand anyway."

But that's exactly where the enemy wants us, alone in our pain, trapped in silence.

Healing, however, doesn't happen in isolation. It happens in communion.

God created us for relationship. From the very beginning, He said it was not good for man to be alone. That wasn't just about marriage. It was about the human condition. We were made to carry one another, to share burdens, and to walk alongside each other, especially when the road gets rough.

As Christians, we believe that the Church is not just a gathering, it is a living Body. When one part suffers, the whole body suffers (cf. 1 Corinthians 12:26). This means your pain isn't a private burden but it's something the Body of Christ is meant to carry with you. The enemy thrives in isolation, but healing happens in communion, whether that's through community, a small group, or simply one trusted soul who can sit with you in your struggle.

There is incredible healing power in simply being heard. When someone listens, really listens, without fixing you, without judging you, without offering clichés, but just *stays* with you in the pain… something sacred happens. That space becomes holy ground.

I experienced this very early in our journey with Couples for Christ. It was just three months after we joined when I attended my first CFC anniversary celebration in Maidenhead. Riza had a meeting up north, so I dropped her off and drove alone to the event, filled with excitement. I was eager to meet all the members of the community from other areas, to finally connect with the brothers and sisters I had heard so much about.

But the moment I stepped into the hotel hall, I felt something shift. Everyone looked so elegant, men in suits, women in beautiful gowns. I came in wearing a shirt, jeans, and rubber shoes. At the registration table, they asked where I was from. When I said "Cardiff," they looked down the list… and didn't find my name. Or any mention of Cardiff at all. They asked me to wait in the corner.

So I waited. And waited.

No one came.

I looked around and saw only unfamiliar faces. No smiles. No sense of welcome. I didn't know anyone. No one seemed to see me. I walked into the bathroom and quietly cried. My heart sank. I felt rejected and alone. I started thinking that maybe this wasn't the community I thought it was. Maybe this wasn't home after all.

I made up my mind to leave. I walked toward the exit, ready to call Riza and tell her I was done. And then I heard a voice.

"*Brother Nash!*"

I turned, and there he was, David Sinclair. He recognised me immediately, called me by name, and smiled with genuine joy. That simple moment changed everything. He welcomed me, brought me inside, and introduced me to others. In that moment, I realised the power of presence and how one person's welcome can undo a thousand moments of loneliness.

Sometimes, we need a friend. Sometimes, a mentor. Sometimes, a priest or spiritual companion. And yes, sometimes a stranger becomes the instrument God uses to remind us we are not alone.

One of the most powerful forms of "letting someone in" is seeking spiritual direction or going to Confession. It's not just about admitting faults, it's about opening our hearts to healing through another person, someone God has called to listen, guide, and pray with us. A priest or spiritual companion can help us recognise where God is moving in our pain, especially when we can't see it ourselves.

Even Jesus didn't carry His cross alone. Simon of Cyrene helped Him. Not because He needed help but because He wanted us to understand that it's okay to receive help too.

Letting people in doesn't always fix the pain. But it reminds us we don't have to carry it alone. That reminder, in itself, is healing.

Jesus never promised that we'd avoid suffering. But He did promise that we'd never suffer alone. When we let others into our pain, when we allow ourselves to be seen, known, and carried, we mirror something sacred. We reflect the love of Christ, who not only bore His own Cross but also entered fully into ours. In those shared moments of vulnerability, healing doesn't always come through answers. It comes through presence. Through someone who stays, who listens, who says, "You don't have to go through this alone."

Grace In The Silence

"Bear one another's burdens, and so you will fulfil the law of Christ."

Galatians 6:2

To bear another's burden is to step into their pain with compassion, not to fix it, but to share in it. It's in these moments that we most closely reflect the heart of Christ, who bore our sins and sufferings as His own. This verse is both a comfort and a call: a comfort in knowing that we are not meant to carry our crosses alone, and a call to be present to others who may be silently struggling. Ask yourself: *Who has God placed around me that I can reach out to? And am I allowing others to carry my burdens, too?*

4.5
Carrying Pain With Purpose

Some pains don't go away quickly. Some losses don't get "fixed." And for those who walk with Christ, that can be hard to accept because we believe in healing, in miracles, in restoration. But there are seasons in life when God doesn't remove the pain... instead, He invites us to carry it with Him.

Not because He wants us to suffer, but because He wants to do something deeper with our suffering.

One of the greatest mysteries of our faith is the idea of *redemptive suffering*, that through our union with Christ, our pain can become a path not just of endurance, but of purpose. We're not asked to simply suffer, we're invited to offer that suffering for others, for the Church, for the world, for our own healing. It's a mystery the saints embraced with radical trust. And it's something we can enter into too, even in small, quiet ways.

We may not always find the reason behind our suffering. But we can always ask: *What can I do with this pain? Who can I offer this for? How can I let this draw me closer to Christ?*

When we offer our suffering, we're not pretending it doesn't hurt. We're not denying the weight of it. We're simply giving it a new direction. We are saying, "Lord, I don't understand this... but I choose to unite it with Your cross. I offer it for someone who needs grace. I offer it for healing I can't yet see."

That prayer echoes Jesus Himself in the Garden of Gethsemane. He cried out, "Father, if You are willing, take this cup from me... yet not my will, but Yours be done"

(Luke 22:42). Even Christ, fully God and fully man, entered into the full depth of human anguish. He didn't glorify pain, but He did choose to love through it. And that choice transformed the Cross from a place of despair into the greatest sign of love the world has ever known.

I've learned that this kind of offering transforms not only the suffering, it transforms the sufferer. We stop being victims of pain and become co-workers in grace. It doesn't make the hurt disappear, but it gives it dignity. It gives it weight in heaven.

Still, let's be honest: some days, it's hard to see the point. Offering our suffering doesn't always come with a clear sense of meaning. And that's okay. Faith doesn't erase confusion. It carries us through it. If you can't find the strength to offer your pain today, don't worry. Just give God your willingness. He will do the rest. Even the smallest surrender becomes a seed of grace in His hands.

And for me, the one person I always lift up in my suffering is my son, Shann.

Everything I face right now, the challenges, the burdens, the inner battles, I go through them willingly and without hesitation, because I offer them all for him. If I could bear what he's carrying, I would do it in a heartbeat. In fact, I often pray that God would just take whatever pain or pressure my son is feeling and place it on me instead. I know I can take it. I know I can survive it.

But what breaks me is seeing him wrestle with the weight of the world.

That's the hardest kind of pain, not your own, but the pain of someone you love more than life itself.

It's in moments like that when redemptive suffering becomes real. It's not just a theological idea. It's a daily offering. A father's quiet prayer at night. A surrender. A cry to heaven: "Lord, use this. Take this. Let it somehow bring healing to him."

And more than that, when we serve others *through* our suffering, healing often begins. We might not feel strong. But sometimes the person sitting next to us needs to see someone *not okay* still showing up. Still loving. Still serving. Sometimes, we don't know how much hope we're giving just by being faithful through the struggle.

This isn't a call to glorify pain. It's a call to bring pain to the cross, and from there, discover how God wants to use it. When we let Him, He never wastes a single tear.

This is the Paschal Mystery at work: in Christ, suffering and death are never the end. They are the passage to resurrection. When we unite our pain with His, we allow God to bring life even from sorrow. Our wounds may remain, but so did His, and through them, He redeemed the world. Your cross, carried with Christ, can become someone else's path to hope. And that is a purpose worth holding onto.

Grace In The Silence

"Now I rejoice in my sufferings for your sake, and in my flesh I complete what is lacking in Christ's afflictions for the sake of his body, that is, the Church."

Colossians 1:24

Our suffering, when united with Christ, participates in His redeeming work. St. Paul isn't saying that Christ's sacrifice was incomplete, but rather, that we are invited to share in its power by offering our own crosses for others. This verse reminds us that pain need not be wasted. It can become intercession. It can become love. When we carry our suffering with purpose, especially for someone else, we become living channels of grace for the Church.

Reflect today: *What pain can I offer, and for whom? Who might need the grace God could release through my hidden suffering?*

4.6
Give Yourself Permission to Rest

When life is difficult, when we are pressed from every side, when we're holding it together for others, rest can feel like a luxury we can't afford.

We keep going. We push through. We stay strong for our families, our ministries, our jobs, our loved ones. And before we know it, we're not just tired. We're worn out in body, in mind, and in spirit.

But here's the truth many of us forget: God did not create us to run endlessly. Even He, after creating the universe, *rested*.

In the biblical tradition, God established the Sabbath not just as a rule, but as a rhythm of grace. The Catechism reminds us that the Sabbath is a day of "protest against the servitude of work and the worship of money" (CCC 2172). In other words, rest is resistance. It says: *I am not a machine. I am a beloved child of God, and I trust Him enough to stop and breathe.*

Sabbath is more than a day, it's a posture of the soul that honours our limits and opens us to grace.

Rest isn't a reward for finishing everything. It's a command. It's an act of trust. When we allow ourselves to rest, we are saying, *"Lord, I believe You are working even when I am not."*

Rest doesn't have to mean taking a long vacation (though that helps, too). Sometimes, it's simply pausing in your day to breathe. To pray. To sit quietly and do nothing for a while without guilt.

And sometimes, the most sacred thing you can do is set a boundary. Rest means learning to say, *"Not right now,"* even to good things. We don't honour God by running ourselves into the ground. We honour Him by stewarding the life and energy He has given us. Rest isn't selfish. It's faithful. When we stop trying to hold everything together, we make space for God to be God.

For me, one of the things that helps me reconnect with that rest is music.

There were countless moments when prayer felt like too much effort. I'd reach for the remote, for Netflix, or for anything that would distract me. I even bought spiritual books thinking they would help, but they just ended up gathering dust. I didn't know where to begin.

But music... music did something that words couldn't.

A song I could relate to, a melody that pierced the silence, would stir something in my soul. Sometimes, that was enough to slowly bring me back into prayer. Not formal. Not polished. Just real. Just present.

Rest can look like that too. Something simple. Something that brings peace. A walk. A nap. Listening to your favourite Christian song on repeat. Letting your body and your spirit breathe again.

I've also found rest in sacred silence. Not just the absence of noise, but the presence of stillness. Turning off the notifications, stepping away from the pressure, and just sitting in God's presence, no agenda, no productivity, just being. In a noisy environment, that kind of rest is healing. Sometimes, the most powerful prayer is simply resting in the awareness that God is with you.

It's okay to step back. It's okay to say no for a while. It's okay to admit that you're tired.

Rest does not mean you are giving up. It means you are allowing God to renew you.

Because even Jesus, after healing and preaching and serving, would retreat to the mountain, or the quiet places, to pray and rest. He was never rushed. He was never frantic. And He invites us to follow His rhythm, not the world's.

So, if you're tired, if you're running on empty. Pause. Not just to recover, but to remember who you are. You are not what you produce. You are not only what you do. You are God's beloved, and He delights in you even when you're resting. Rest is not stepping away from your mission. Rather, it's stepping into God's care, so you can live and love from a place of renewal.

Pain can overwhelm, isolate, and paralyse, but it does not have to define us. In this chapter, we explored tangible, grace-filled ways to navigate suffering while staying grounded in faith and community.

We began by embracing the importance of **showing up**, even when we don't feel ready. Healing often starts by taking that first, imperfect step. Then we talked about the value of **prayer**, not as a performance, but as presence. Whether it's through silence, song, or simple words, prayer is where we reconnect with the God who listens even when we have nothing left to say.

We remembered the power of the **Sacraments**, especially the Eucharist. In Christ's broken body and poured-out blood, we find a mirror of our own brokenness, now transformed into grace. The Eucharist doesn't erase the pain, but it gives us the strength to bear it with meaning.

We also reflected on the importance of **letting people in**, reminding ourselves that healing often comes through human connection. Community is not perfect, but it is God's way of helping us carry what we were never meant to bear alone.

We learned about **carrying pain with purpose**, the mystery of redemptive suffering. Our pain, when united with Christ's, becomes more than just something we endure. It becomes a holy offering. And for many of us, offering that pain for someone we love brings deeper healing than we expected.

Finally, we were reminded to **rest**. To slow down. To let go of the pressure to keep performing or producing. Rest is not a weakness, it's a sacred act of trust in God's care. Even Jesus stepped away to renew His strength. So must we.

If there's one message this chapter leaves us with, it's this:

You are not alone.

Your pain is seen.

And there is always grace for the next step.

Grace In The Silence

"Come to me, all you who labour and are burdened, and I will give you rest. Take my yoke upon you and learn from me, for I am meek and humble of heart; and you will find rest for your souls."

Matthew 11:28–29

This is not just a gentle invitation, it is a personal call from the heart of Christ to the weary soul. Jesus does not ask us to come when we're strong or sorted out. He asks us to come when we're tired, anxious, overworked, and overwhelmed. His rest is not mere escape, it is restoration. To take His yoke is to walk beside Him, to let Him carry what we cannot, and to learn His rhythm, meekness, humility, and trust. This rest doesn't always change our circumstances, but it changes our hearts.

Today, ask yourself: *Am I carrying burdens I was never meant to carry alone? What would it look like to lay them down at the feet of Christ, today, even for just a moment?*

4.7
When You Ask God for Something

We often come before God in prayer with longing and hoping for a change, asking for healing, seeking answers. And many times, we ask with sincere hearts. But how often do we pause to consider how God answers?

We expect outcomes. God offers transformation.

We want a solution. God gives us a journey.

Think of Abraham, who waited decades for the fulfilment of God's promise. Or Moses, who asked to enter the Promised Land but was shown it from a distance. Or Mary, who said yes to God's will not knowing it would lead her to a Cross. Scripture is full of people who asked, waited, wrestled, and were changed in the process. Their lives weren't made easier, but they were made holier. God's answers were rarely immediate, but they were always faithful.

Sometimes, God's answer to our every prayer is a **clear yes**. A door opens, an opportunity presents itself, healing comes, peace returns. Other times, it's **a patient wait**. Not because God is ignoring us, but because the soil is not yet ready to support a flourishing plant. And then there are times when His answer is simply **no**, not out of cruelty or silence, but because what we're asking may not lead us to holiness, or because something far better lies ahead.

But here's what many of us overlook: when God answers, He rarely does so by dropping the result into our laps. He invites us into the process.

When we pray for strength, He allows the weight to be heavy. When we pray for patience, He sends delay.

I've lived this in my own journey. When I turned my back on the Church, I wasn't looking for a way back. I thought I had already found my answers elsewhere. But beneath my atheism and anger, I believe someone, maybe Riza, maybe others, was praying for me. I didn't feel a sudden change. What I felt instead was tension, questions, restlessness. I asked for peace, but God first exposed everything that was unsettled within me. I thought I was searching for meaning; God was leading me to Himself. It took years and it didn't come in the form I expected. But looking back now, I see it clearly: God wasn't ignoring my cries. He was answering them by slowly reshaping my heart.

When we pray to love better, He surrounds us with people who are hard to love.

When we ask for peace, He might expose the restlessness in our hearts first.

This is not punishment. It's formation. It's the loving discipline of a Father who is more interested in our holiness than our comfort.

Prayer is not a transaction. It's a relationship. It's not about persuading God to give us what we want, but about opening our hearts so He can give us what we *need*. Often, the greatest fruit of prayer isn't the change in our circumstances but the change in our character. The more we pray, the more we are conformed to the heart of Christ. Learning to trust even when we don't understand, to surrender even when we long for control.

And the truth is: we often don't recognise the answer to our prayer until we've been changed by it.

So if you're still waiting, still praying, still longing, don't give up. God has not forgotten you. Sometimes the silence is the space where He is doing His most delicate work. Trust that every sincere prayer is heard, every tear is counted, and every season has purpose. And even if His answer isn't what you expected, it will always be what draws you closer to Him.

Grace In The Silence

"Before I was afflicted I went astray, but now I keep your word."

Psalm 119:67

Take a moment to reflect:

- What have you been asking God for lately?

- Can you see how He might already be answering, not in the way you expected, but in ways that stretch and shape you?

- What if your current discomfort is God's very answer to your prayer?

In silence, thank God for not just the answers, but for the path He's drawing you into. Ask for the grace to trust the process, even when it's difficult.

EPILOGUE
The Wounds That Speak Of Love

Pain never leaves us the same.

It either breaks us or transforms us. It can harden our hearts or deepen our compassion. And often, the difference lies in *who* we walk with in the midst of it.

This book was never written from a place of resolution, but from the middle of the journey. I don't have all the answers. I still carry questions, scars, and moments when faith feels like a whisper in the dark. But I've also found that even in the silence, *God is there*. Not always in the way I expect, but always in the way I need.

If there's one thing pain has taught me, it's this: our wounds are not useless. They can become windows through which grace enters. And when we offer them to God, He doesn't just patch us up. He reshapes us, breathes new life into our broken places, and often uses our healing to heal others.

So if you are hurting as you read these final words, know this:

You are not abandoned.

Your pain is not wasted. And this is not the end of your story.

ALSO BY THE AUTHOR

1. SION : 1

THE BOY WHO BARELY SPEAKS

2. SION :2

THE WHISPERING CHRONICLES

REFLECTION GUIDE

Here are some personal reflection questions you can use alone or with a small group

Chapter 1 – The Meaning of Pain

- How has your understanding of pain changed over the years?
- Can you name a moment when pain led to unexpected growth?

Chapter 2 – Why Do People Experience Pain?

- Have you ever questioned God in your suffering? What did you discover?
- How do you now see the relationship between free will, sin, and suffering?

Chapter 3 – No Other Way But Pain

- What is one painful experience that, in hindsight, shaped your character or faith?
- Can you see how that pain led to a deeper trust in God?

Chapter 4 – Practical Guides to Overcoming Pain

- Which of the six guides in Chapter 4 spoke most to you? Why?
- Is there someone you need to let in during your time of struggle?
- Are you offering your pain for someone else? What intention do you carry in your suffering?

CLOSING PRAYER

Lord God,

You who see the hidden ache in every heart, I come before You not with strength,

but with trembling hands and tear-stained prayers. You know my story.

You've walked with me through every storm,

even when I didn't feel You, even when I stopped speaking to You.

Today, I place before You all the pain the wounds I hide, the questions I carry, and the hopes I'm afraid to hope again. Redeem what was lost. Heal what was broken. Transform what still feels raw and unresolved.

Give me the grace to walk forward, to find meaning in the struggle,

and to be a source of comfort for others who are still in their valley.

May I never forget the power of Your Cross the place where love and suffering met, and where death gave way to resurrection.

Jesus, wounded yet risen, I unite my pain with Yours. Use it for something holy.

Amen.

Published in Collaboration with Noble Legacy Publishing

www.noblelegacypublishing.co.uk

www.ingramcontent.com/pod-product-compliance
Lightning Source LLC
Chambersburg PA
CBHW061233070526
44584CB00030B/4102